Weatherwise

Snow and Blizzards

Robyn Hardyman

WAYLAND

Published in paperback in 2014 by Wayland
Copyright © Wayland 2014

Wayland, 338 Euston Road, London NW1 3BH
Wayland Australia, Level 17/207 Kent Street, Sydney, NSW 2000

British Library Cataloguing in Publication Data
Hardyman, Robyn
Snow and blizzards. – (Weatherwise)
1. Snow – Juvenile literature 2. Blizzards – Juvenile literature
I. Title
551.5'784

Produced for Wayland by Calcium
Design: Rob Norridge and Paul Myerscough
Editor: Sarah Eason
Editor for Wayland: Claire Shanahan
Illustrations: Geoff Ward
Photography by Tudor Photography
Picture research: Maria Joannou
Consultant: Harold Pratt

ISBN 978 0 7502 8144 7

1 3 5 7 9 10 8 6 4 2

Alamy Images: David Grossman 14; **Dreamstime:** Martine Oger 27, Sampete 21; **Fotolia:** Waring D 6; **Istockphoto:** Milan Klusacek 13; **Photolibrary:** Index Stock Imagery/Yvette Cardozo 16; **Photoshot:** EyePress 26; **Rex Features:** David Heerde 10, Dennis Stone 25; **Shutterstock**: Francois Arseneault 20, Michael Bauer 23, Jack Dagley Photography 1, 11, Dark O 4, Dainis Derics 18, Vladimirs Koskins 12, Denis Miraniuk 19, George Muresan 17, Mikhail Pogosov 22, Tony Sanchez-Espinosa 24, Kristian Sekulic 9, Urosr 15.

Cover photograph: **Shutterstock** (Kristian Sekulic)

Wayland is a division of Hachette Children's Books, an Hachette UK company.
www.hachette.co.uk

Contents

What is snow?

Snow is made up of millions of snowflakes
that fall to the Earth from a cloud. It is
part of the weather. Weather describes
the conditions outside at a particular time,
for example, whether it is sunny or raining.

The highest mountains have
snow on their peaks, even in hot
countries, such as Kenya in Africa.

Snowflakes are **crystals** of frozen water. They form when the air is cold. Water droplets in a cloud join together with ice crystals or dust, and then freeze. Usually, these crystals melt as they fall, and reach the ground as rain. But, if the air is cold enough, they stay frozen and fall as snow.

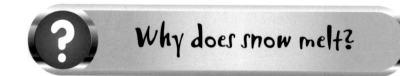

Why does snow melt?

The warmth of the Sun melts snow. Where the Sun does not shine on snow, the snow lasts longer. In places where the air is really cold, snow never melts.

This diagram shows the water cycle. Water normally falls from clouds as rain during the cycle. However, when the air is very cold, it falls as snow instead.

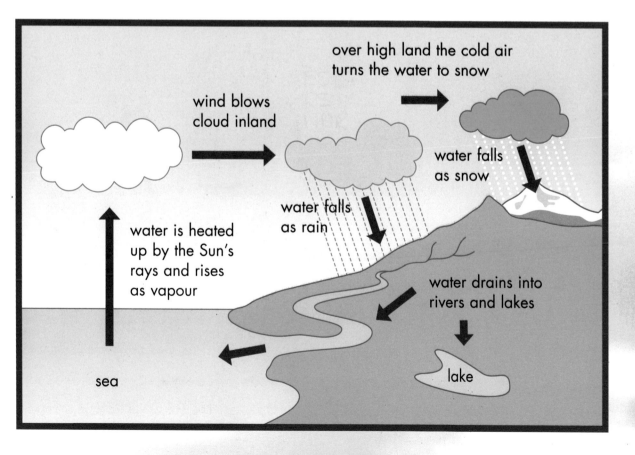

over high land the cold air turns the water to snow

wind blows cloud inland

water falls as snow

water falls as rain

water is heated up by the Sun's rays and rises as vapour

water drains into rivers and lakes

sea

lake

A snowy world

Snow can fall anywhere on Earth. For snow to fall, the air has to be very cold and contain **moisture**. The snow melts when the weather warms up.

A severe snow storm is called a **blizzard**. This is when strong winds blow as the snow falls. Blizzards occur most often in the middle of large continents, such as Europe, North America and Asia.

Snow falls most frequently during winter in northern countries, such as Canada. Here, a thick blanket of snow can cover the land.

This map shows the parts of the world in which the ground is covered with snow all year.

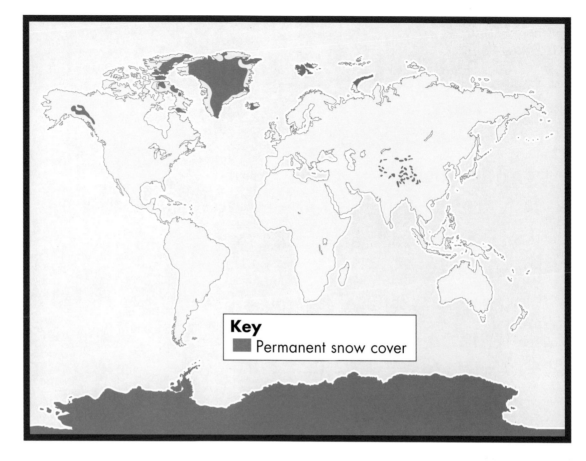

Key
Permanent snow cover

Some parts of the Earth are always cold, even in summer. The coldest areas are the North and South Poles. This is the Arctic and Antarctic. There is a lot of ice in these areas for most of the year, but it does not snow there all the time. This is because there is very little moisture in the air. When it does snow, there is usually a blizzard.

? Where is the coldest place on Earth?

The coldest temperature ever was recorded in Vostock Station, Antarctica. In 1983, the temperature there dropped to −89° Celsius!

7

Snowflakes

No snowflake is the same. Every snowflake is slightly different from all other snowflakes.

All snowflakes have six sides or points, but they have different shapes. Some snowflakes are star-shaped. Others look like needles, columns or blocks. The shape of a snowflake affects how quickly it falls to the ground.

These are the six most common snowflake shapes.

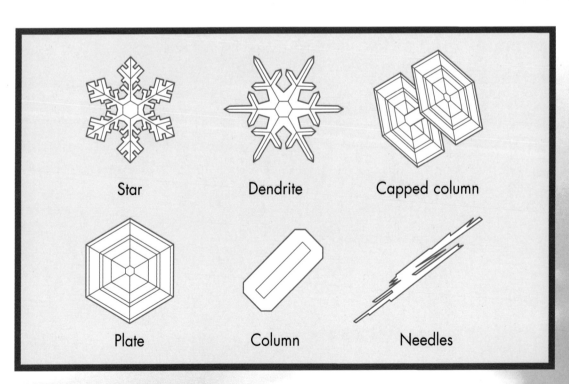

Star   Dendrite   Capped column

Plate   Column   Needles

Snowflakes vary in size. Some are also wetter than others. When the air contains a lot of moisture, many ice crystals form. These join together to make large snowflakes. They fall as 'wet' snow. This type of snow is good for making snowballs.

When it is much colder, the air contains less moisture. Fewer ice crystals form, and the snowflakes are smaller. They fall as drier, powdery snow. This is the type of snow that is found in a blizzard. Very tiny snowflakes are called 'diamond dust'.

Dry, powdery snow is the best kind for skiing.

Sleet and hail

Cold weather often brings snow. It can also bring other weather conditions, including **sleet**, hail and **freezing rain**.

Sleet is rain that freezes to tiny pieces of ice before it reaches the ground. Sleet usually forms when the temperature is just above freezing.

Sleet can cover the roads with a layer of ice, making them dangerous to drive on.

Hail is frozen raindrops. These are little lumps of ice that form in thunderclouds. They are formed when strong **air currents** carry water droplets up into the coldest parts of the cloud. There, they freeze and are tossed up and down, so they become coated with ice. These icy lumps then fall to Earth as heavy hailstones.

Sometimes enormous hailstones can fall during freak storms. These hailstones can be as big as golfballs.

Living with snow

People who live in cold areas have to be prepared for snow and ice. Unless the snow is very bad, they still go to school and work.

Snow can make paths and driveways slippery and difficult to walk on. People sometimes sprinkle salt, sand or cat litter on them to melt snow and ice.

In many Russian cities, people are used to heavy snowfall in winter. Daily life continues as normal.

Some people have jobs relating to snowy weather. Drivers of special trucks sprinkle **grit** and salt on the roads, to make the snow melt when it falls. After a snowfall, drivers of **snowploughs** try to clear large **snowdrifts** from the roads. Other workers rescue people who have been stranded in their houses.

In places where there is heavy snowfall, people may have to dig a path through the snow from their house to the road.

 What is a snowdrift?

A snowdrift is a large pile of snow. Snowdrifts are made when there is heavy snow and the wind blows it against objects, such as walls. Snowdrifts can block roads and railways, so cars, buses and trains cannot be used.

Dressing for warmth

People wear special clothes and footwear to keep them warm in cold, snowy weather. They often put on several layers of lightweight clothes. This keeps them warmer than wearing heavy clothes.

When people go outdoors in the snow, they may wear a waterproof jacket so they stay dry. Water-resistant boots, lined with material, may be worn over warm socks.

Elderly people are particularly vulnerable to the cold. It is especially important that they wear warm clothing when it is cold outside.

Mountaineers have to wear special clothing to protect themselves from extreme cold.

A lot of body heat is lost through the head, so it is important to wear a hat when it is cold and snowy. People wear mittens to keep their hands warm, too. A scarf worn over the mouth and nose protects people's lungs from the cold air and snowflakes.

? What happens if people get too cold?

If people get too cold, they can get **hypothermia** or **frostbite**. Hypothermia is when someone's body temperature becomes dangerously low. Frostbite is a condition in which the blood supply to the outer parts of the body becomes cut off. In extreme cases, the skin of affected areas may turn black and become infected.

Is snow useful?

Despite the problems it can cause, snow can be useful. Snow is a great **insulator**. This means that it keeps in the heat. A thick layer of snow keeps the ground warm. It acts like a blanket, protecting plant seeds and roots, and the burrows of small animals, from damage by the cold above ground.

Because snow keeps heat in, it is good for building shelters called **igloos**. The Inuit people in the Arctic can build an igloo from blocks of firm snow in about an hour.

The Inuit word 'igloo' means 'snow hut'.

Snow can be a useful supply of water in hot, dry countries that have mountains. The snow on the mountains melts in spring and summer, and the water flows into rivers. Some rivers, such as the River Nile in Africa, would dry up in summer without water from melting snow on nearby mountains.

People can also have great fun in the snow! Snow sports include snowboarding and sledging.

People could not build snowmen without snow!

What is a blizzard?

A blizzard is a storm that takes place during heavy snowfall, strong winds and very cold temperatures. Blizzards are the most severe form of snowy weather.

The strong wind in a blizzard blows the snow into deep snowdrifts. These can block doorways and even buildings. Blowing snow makes it impossible to see beyond about 200 metres.

People hurry home to shelter indoors during a blizzard.

Sometimes, strong winds come after a snowfall. This is called a ground blizzard. Loose snow or ice on the ground is lifted and blown around by high winds. Ground blizzards occur in large areas of flat, open land.

In a ground blizzard, wind can blow the snow into strange shapes and patterns that look like waves.

19

Deadly blizzards

Blizzards can be very dangerous. They can bring down electricity and telephone lines. They can trap people in cars, buses and trains. Occasionally, people have frozen to death in a blizzard.

People should never go out in a blizzard. It is safer to stay inside. If someone becomes caught in a blizzard, they should try to find shelter, for example, in a hotel or restaurant.

Helicopters may be needed to rescue people who are trapped during a blizzard.

In places where blizzards often occur, drivers should carry a safety kit. They should have a shovel to dig themselves out of snowdrifts. Brightly coloured cloth can be made into a **distress flag**. Blankets, a torch, and food and drinks, are important, too.

Blizzards can bring traffic to a standstill.

21

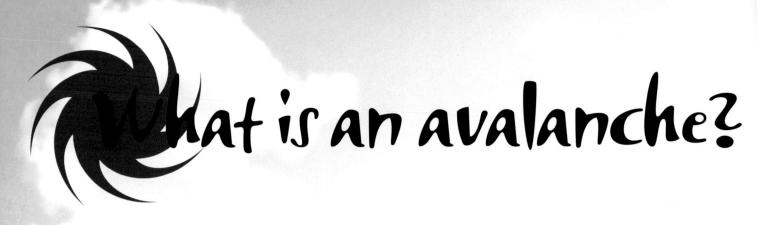

What is an avalanche?

An **avalanche** is when soft snow and ice at the top of a mountain breaks away and crashes down the slopes. This sometimes happens if the weather around the mountain suddenly gets warmer. An avalanche can also be caused when there is too much thick, heavy snow on a slope.

An avalanche can travel at up to 400 kilometres per hour.

Thousands of avalanches happen on mountains every year. Everything in the path of an avalanche – people, animals, trees and buildings – is buried by the snow.

Sometimes, explosions are deliberately set off in the mountains to make any loose snow fall away. That way, it never becomes thick enough to cause an avalanche.

Avalanches happen most often on steep slopes. If trees on the mountain look bent or damaged, this is a sign that there has been an avalanche there.

People should ring an avalanche centre before they go up a mountain to see if there is a risk of an avalanche happening in the area.

Ski resorts prevent people from skiing where an avalanche may occur.

What is a whiteout?

A **whiteout** is an extreme kind of blizzard. Whiteouts occur most often in major storms that produce dry, powdery snow. The heavy snow combines with strong winds, making it almost impossible to see anything. This can be extremely dangerous.

In a whiteout, drivers cannot see the road or other vehicles around them. The strong winds blow the snow into large snowdrifts. These can hide road signs and dangers on the road.

It can be difficult for drivers to judge distances between themselves and other cars during a whiteout, making driving very dangerous.

In a whiteout, people who are walking can lose their sense of direction. They can quickly get lost. Mountain climbers and skiers are unable to see the dangers and obstacles in front of them.

Aircraft may run into difficulties during a whiteout. There may be a build-up of ice on their wings, making it dangerous to fly or land.

It may be too dangerous for planes to fly during a whiteout. Passengers can be stranded at an airport for days while they wait for the snow to clear.

Unbelievable!

In 1979, a plane carrying sightseers to Antarctica crashed into a mountain during whiteout conditions. More than 250 people were killed.

Clearing up

After heavy snow, people have to work hard to bring life back to normal. A lot of mess may be left behind, and clearing up can take a long time. Houses, schools and other buildings may need to be repaired. Snow and ice have to be cleared from driveways, paths and roads.

Telephone and electricity lines may need to be repaired after heavy snowfall.

Trucks spread salt and grit on the roads to melt the snow and ice. They may need to put **snow chains** on their tyres so that they can grip the road. Snowploughs and **snow blowers** clear the roads. Snowploughs work best with wet snow, while snow blowers suck up deep, dry snow and blow it away from the road.

Snowploughs clear motorways and main roads before they clear smaller roads.

What happens if people are stranded?

In a blizzard, villages may be cut off by massive snowdrifts and the people there stranded. Small planes or helicopters drop emergency supplies, such as food and water, to help them until the roads are cleared.

Measuring melting ice

How long does an ice cube take to melt? It all depends where it is! Follow this experiment to find out how quickly or slowly ice melts on different materials.

You will need:
- two identical china bowls
- tin foil
- tray of ice cubes
- pencil
- piece of A4 paper
- ruler
- bubble wrap
- waxed paper

1. Copy the chart onto a piece of paper.

	Ice cube 1 size before experiment	Ice cube 1 size after experiment		Ice cube 2 size before experiment	Ice cube 2 size after experiment	Why did the ice cubes melt at different rates?
Tin foil	X		Bowl	Y		
Bubble wrap			Bowl			
Waxed paper			Bowl			

2. Measure the height and width of two identical ice cubes. Record your findings on your chart: in box X for ice cube 1 and box Y for ice cube 2.

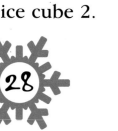
28

3. Line one of your bowls with tin foil. Place one ice cube inside it.

4. Place the second ice cube inside the second bowl. Place both bowls side by side. Leave for 90 minutes.

5. Return to the bowls. Measure each ice cube as you did in step 2, recording your findings on your chart.

6. Compare your findings on your chart. Did one ice cube melt more quickly than the other? Why do you think this was? Record your reasons on the chart.

7. Try the same experiment with bubble wrap and waxed paper. Remember to record your findings on your chart and compare the results. Why do you think the ice cubes melt at different rates when you use different materials?

Bubble wrap

Waxed paper

Glossary

air current movement of air in a particular direction

avalanche when a thick layer of snow falls down a mountainside

blizzard storm with heavy snow and strong winds

crystals small shapes of frozen water

distress flag flag someone waves to attract attention when in danger

freezing rain when rain freezes as it touches the ground

frostbite when the skin and flesh freeze and die

grit very small pieces of stone or sand

hypothermia when the body temperature falls to a dangerously low
level causing shivering, sleepiness, dizziness and, eventually, death

igloo shelter made from blocks of firm snow

insulator material or substance that is able to keep in heat

moisture tiny drops of water in the air

sleet rain that freezes as tiny ice pellets before it reaches the ground

snowdrifts thick piles of snow blown by the wind

snow blower vehicle that sucks up snow and blows it away
from roads

snow chain special chain that attaches to tyres, so a vehicle does
not slip on ice or snow

snowplough vehicle that pushes snow off roads

whiteout extreme blizzard with heavy snow and strong winds

wind chill factor effect of a strong wind making the air
temperature feel colder than it actually is

Find out more

Books

Rain and Snow (Measuring the Weather) by Angella Streluk and Alan Rodgers (Heinemann Library, 2007)

Weather Around You: Snow by Anita Ganeri (Wayland, 2007)

Weather (Earthwise) by Jim Pipe (Franklin Watts, 2008)

Weather Patterns (Geography Detective Investigates) by Jen Green (Wayland 2009)

Websites

For lots more information about snow go to:
www.bbc.co.uk/weather/weatherwise/factfiles/ basics/precipitation_snow.shtml

This children's site has lots of information about snow and blizzards:
www.kidzworld.com/article/1587-all-about-snowflakes

For some great images of snow visit:
www.rmets.org/cloudbank/index.php

Index